Better Homes and Gardens®

EASY MICROWAVE MEALS

Our seal assures you that every recipe in *Easy Microwave Meals*
has been tested in the Better Homes and Gardens® Test Kitchen.
This means that each recipe is practical and reliable,
and meets our high standards of taste appeal.

For years, Better Homes and Gardens® Books has been a leader in publishing cook books. In *Easy Microwave Meals,* we've pulled together a delicious collection of recipes from several of our latest best-sellers. These no-fail recipes will make your cooking easier and more enjoyable.

Editor: Rosemary C. Hutchinson
Editorial Project Manager: James D. Blume
Graphic Designer: Harijs Priekulis
Electronic Text Processor: Paula Forest

On the front cover: Salami-Vegetable Bake *(see recipe, page 7)*

Contents

3 medium zucchini, sliced lengthwise ¼ inch thick 2 tablespoons water	● Place zucchini and water in a 10x6x2-inch baking dish, then cover with vented clear plastic wrap. Micro-cook on 100% power (HIGH) 4 to 6 minutes or till zucchini is crisp-tender, rearranging zucchini once. Drain well, then pat dry with a paper towel. Set aside.
1 pound bulk Italian sausage 1 small onion, chopped ½ of a 15½-ounce can (1 cup) meatless spaghetti sauce ⅓ cup ready-to-cook couscous	● Crumble sausage into a 1½-quart casserole, then stir in onion. Micro-cook covered, on 100% power (HIGH) 4½ to 5½ minutes or till the sausage is no longer pink and onion is tender, stirring once to break up sausage. Drain off fat. Stir in the spaghetti sauce and couscous.
1 slightly beaten egg ¾ cup low-fat cottage cheese 2 tablespoons grated Parmesan cheese 1 cup shredded mozzarella cheese (4 ounces)	● In a small bowl combine egg, cottage cheese, and Parmesan cheese. Arrange *half* of the zucchini in the 10x6x2-inch baking dish. Top with egg mixture, then *half* of the sausage mixture. Top with remaining zucchini and sausage mixture. Cover with vented clear plastic wrap. Micro-cook on 100% power (HIGH) 8 to 10 minutes or till heated through, rotating the dish a half-turn twice. Sprinkle mozzarella cheese atop. Let stand, uncovered, for 5 minutes. Makes 6 servings.

Surprise, no pasta! Instead of noodles you use zucchini cut into long, thin strips. Remember to thoroughly drain the precooked zucchini on paper towels so it doesn't water out during cooking.

Peppered Beef

1 10-ounce package frozen
  brussels sprouts
¾ pound beef top round
  steak
1 tablespoon cooking oil

● Thaw brussels sprouts. Cut in half. Thinly bias-slice beef into bite-size strips.
  Preheat a 10-inch microwave browning dish on 100% power (HIGH) for 5 minutes. Add oil to browning dish, then swirl to coat dish. Add beef. Micro-cook, uncovered, on 100% power (HIGH) for 2 to 3 minutes or till done, stirring once. Use a slotted spoon to remove beef and reserve juices. Set aside.

For easier slicing, put the meat in the freezer until it's firm but not hard— about 45 minutes. If the meat is already frozen, just partially thaw it.

⅓ cup dry sherry
¼ cup water
¼ cup soy sauce
¾ to 1 teaspoon crushed
  whole black pepper
2 cloves garlic, minced
2 medium carrots, thinly
  sliced (1 cup)

● Meanwhile, in a small bowl stir together sherry, water, soy sauce, pepper, and garlic. Stir into reserved juices. Add brussels sprouts and carrots. Micro-cook, covered, on 100% power (HIGH) for 5 to 7 minutes or till vegetables are crisp-tender.

2 tablespoons cold water
2 teaspoons cornstarch
  Hot cooked noodles *or*
  spaetzle

● Stir water into cornstarch. Stir into vegetable mixture. Micro-cook, uncovered, on 100% power (HIGH) for 2 to 4 minutes or till thickened and bubbly, stirring every minute. Stir in beef. Micro-cook, uncovered, on 100% power (HIGH) for 2 to 3 minutes or till heated through. Serve over noodles or spaetzle. Makes 4 servings.

To bias-slice, hold a sharp knife or cleaver at a 45-degree angle to the cutting board while you thinly slice the meat. If the meat slices are large, cut them into bite-size pieces.

Salami-Vegetable Bake

Also pictured on the cover.

4 medium potatoes, peeled and sliced
2 carrots, sliced (1 cup)
1 medium onion, sliced
⅓ cup water
¼ teaspoon minced dried garlic
3 cups shredded cabbage

● In a 2-quart casserole combine the potatoes, carrots, onion, water, and garlic. Micro-cook, covered, on 100% power (HIGH) about 10 minutes or till vegetables are crisp-tender, stirring after 5 minutes. Stir in cabbage.

½ cup hot water
2½ teaspoons instant beef bouillon granules
1½ teaspoons caraway seed
2 tablespoons all-purpose flour
1 8-ounce carton plain yogurt *or* dairy sour cream

● Stir together water, bouillon granules, and caraway till granules are dissolved. Add to vegetable mixture. Micro-cook, covered, on 100% power (HIGH) 4½ minutes, stirring once.
  Stir flour into yogurt or sour cream. Stir into vegetable mixture. Micro-cook, uncovered, on 100% power (HIGH) 2 minutes, stirring once. Stir again.

2 4-ounce packages thin-sliced hard salami

● Fold the salami into quarters, then arrange around outer edge of the casserole, pressing salami into vegetable mixture. Micro-cook, uncovered, on 100% power (HIGH) 2½ minutes. Spoon off fat. Serves 6.

Corny Calico Casseroles

| 2 teaspoons butter *or* margarine
½ cup cornbread stuffing mix | ● In a small bowl micro-cook butter or margarine, uncovered, on 100% power (HIGH) 30 to 40 seconds or till melted. Toss with stuffing mix, then set aside. |

| 1 cup frozen whole kernel corn
½ of a small sweet red *or* green pepper, chopped
2 tablespoons sliced green onion
1 tablespoon butter *or* margarine | ● In a 1-quart casserole combine corn, pepper, green onion, and butter or margarine. Micro-cook, covered, on 100% power (HIGH) about 3 minutes or till pepper is crisp-tender. |

| 2 eggs
¼ cup milk
¼ teaspoon Worcestershire sauce
Dash pepper
¼ pound cooked Polish sausage, chopped
½ cup shredded Swiss cheese (2 ounces) | ● In a 2-cup measure beat together eggs, milk, Worcestershire, and pepper slightly with a fork. Stir egg mixture, sausage, and cheese into corn mixture. Spoon into two 15-ounce casseroles. Sprinkle stuffing mixture on top. Micro-cook, uncovered, on 100% power (HIGH) 6 to 7 minutes or till almost set. Let stand 2 minutes. Serves 2. |

One of our food editors suggested the title for this dish. "The bits of corn, pepper, and sausage make these look like calico casseroles," she said.

Ham and Rye Strata

2 slices day-old rye bread, cut into bite-size cubes
1 cup diced fully cooked ham
½ cup shredded Swiss cheese (2 ounces)
½ cup milk
2 beaten eggs
¼ teaspoon caraway seed (optional)
⅛ teaspoon dry mustard
⅛ teaspoon pepper

● Combine bread and ham. Divide *half* of the bread and ham between 2 individual round 10-ounce casseroles. Reserve remaining bread and ham. Sprinkle cheese atop ham and bread. Micro-cook milk, uncovered, on 100% power (HIGH) 1 to 2 minutes or till hot (180°), but *not* boiling. In a 1-cup measure gradually stir milk into eggs. Stir in caraway seed, if desired; dry mustard; and pepper.

For a strata to be a strata, you must have the layers. Usually stratas include a layer of bread and sliced or shredded cheese bound together with a sauce or egg mixture.

1 slice Swiss cheese, cut into 8 narrow strips (1 ounce)

● Pour *half* of the milk mixture over cheese in each casserole. Top with remaining bread and ham. Micro-cook, covered, on 50% power (MEDIUM) 6 to 8 minutes or till almost set, rotating twice. Arrange cheese atop. Let stand 5 minutes. Serves 2.

No-Measure Beef Stew

1 pound beef stew meat, cut into ½-inch cubes

2 medium sweet potatoes, peeled and cut into 1-inch pieces

2 medium parsnips, peeled and cut into ½-inch pieces

1 medium onion, sliced and separated into rings

1 15-ounce can tomato-herb sauce

1 large green pepper, cut into thin strips

● In a 3-quart casserole combine beef, sweet potatoes, parsnips, and onion. Stir in tomato-herb sauce. Use tomato-herb sauce can to measure ½ can *water*. Stir into vegetable mixture. Micro-cook, covered, on 100% power (HIGH) about 7 minutes or till bubbly; stir. Reduce power to 50% (MEDIUM). Micro-cook, covered, 45 to 50 minutes more or till meat is tender, stirring twice.

● Stir in green pepper. Micro-cook, covered, on 50% power (MEDIUM) about 5 minutes more or till green pepper is crisp-tender. Skim off fat. Stir before serving. Makes 6 to 8 servings.

Faux Polish Hunter's Stew

½ **pound boneless pork, cut into ½-inch cubes** 1 **medium onion, chopped (½ cup)** ½ **pound fully cooked Polish sausage, sliced ½ inch thick**	● In a 2-quart casserole combine pork and onion. Micro-cook, covered, on 100% power (HIGH) 3½ minutes, stirring once. Add sausage. Micro-cook, covered, on 100% power (HIGH) 1½ minutes. Drain well.
½ **cup water** ¼ **cup dry red wine** ½ **teaspoon salt** ½ **teaspoon instant beef bouillon granules** ¼ **teaspoon ground allspice** **Dash pepper** 1 **bay leaf**	● Stir in water, wine, salt, bouillon granules, allspice, and pepper. Add bay leaf. Micro-cook, covered, on 100% power (HIGH) 5 minutes; stir. Reduce power to 50% (MEDIUM). Micro-cook, covered, 5 minutes, stirring once. Remove bay leaf.
1½ **cups shredded cabbage** 1 **8-ounce can sauerkraut, rinsed and drained** 1 **7½-ounce can tomatoes, cut up**	● Stir in the cabbage, sauerkraut, and *undrained* tomatoes. Micro-cook, covered, on 50% power (MEDIUM) 15 minutes, stirring once.
1 **medium apple, chopped (1 cup)** 1 **4½-ounce jar sliced mushrooms, drained**	● Stir in the apple and mushrooms. Micro-cook, covered, on 50% power (MEDIUM) 5 to 10 minutes or till pork is no longer pink and cabbage is tender, stirring once.
1 **tablespoon cornstarch** 1 **tablespoon cold water**	● Combine cornstarch and water, then stir into pork mixture. Micro-cook, uncovered, on 100% power (HIGH) 1 to 2 minutes or till thickened and bubbly, stirring once. Makes 4 servings.

In Poland years ago, hungry hunters came home to a hearty helping of bigos, a stew that's the national dish. The stew varied with the takes of the day and was even made with bear meat. Because bear meat is probably hard to find in your local supermarket, we thought you might prefer using Polish sausage and pork.

Blaze-of-Glory Chili

1 **pound ground beef**	● Crumble ground beef into a 2-quart casserole, then stir in onion, green pepper, and garlic. Micro-cook, covered, on 100% power (HIGH) 5 to 6 minutes or till beef is done, stirring once to break up meat. Drain.
1 **medium onion, chopped (½ cup)**	
1 **small green pepper, seeded and chopped (½ cup)**	
1 **clove garlic, minced**	

1 **15-ounce can red kidney beans, drained**	● Stir in kidney beans; *undrained* tomatoes; soup; chili powder; red pepper, if desired; pepper; and bay leaf. Micro-cook, covered, on 100% power (HIGH) 5 minutes; stir. Reduce power to 50% (MEDIUM). Micro-cook, covered, 20 minutes, stirring twice. Remove bay leaf. Makes 4 or 5 servings.
1 **14½-ounce can tomatoes, cut up**	
1 **10¾-ounce can condensed tomato soup**	
2 **teaspoons chili powder**	
1 **to 1½ teaspoons ground red pepper (optional)**	
⅛ **teaspoon pepper**	
1 **bay leaf**	

Attention stout-hearted chili fans. Here's a fiery version you can spice up or down to suit your taste. To give your mouth a break from the spiciness that builds with every spoonful, add a topper such as crushed crackers, shredded cheese, chopped carrot, sour cream, chopped green pepper, alfalfa sprouts, or chopped fresh tomato.

It's-a-Spicy-Spaghetti Casserole

5 **ounces spaghetti**	● Cook spaghetti according to package directions. Drain. Meanwhile, crumble sausage into a 1½-quart casserole, then stir in onion, celery, and garlic. Micro-cook, covered, on 100% power (HIGH) 5 to 6 minutes or till sausage is no longer pink and onion is tender, stirring once. Drain. Stir in tomato-herb sauce, mushrooms, chili powder, and pepper.
1 **pound bulk Italian sausage**	
1 **medium onion, chopped**	
1 **stalk celery, thinly sliced**	
1 **clove garlic, minced**	
1 **15-ounce can tomato-herb sauce**	
1 **4-ounce can sliced mushrooms, drained**	
2 **teaspoons chili powder**	
¼ **teaspoon crushed red pepper**	

1 **cup shredded mozzarella cheese (4 ounces)**	● Layer *half* of the spaghetti in a 10x6x2-inch baking dish, then top with *half* of the sausage mixture. Repeat layers. Cover with vented clear plastic wrap. Micro-cook on 100% power (HIGH) 8 to 10 minutes or till heated through, rotating the dish a half-turn once. Sprinkle with cheese. Micro-cook, uncovered, on 100% power (HIGH) 30 to 60 seconds or till cheese is melted. Sprinkle with parsley, if desired. Makes 4 to 6 servings.
2 **tablespoons snipped parsley (optional)**	

Much of the spiciness in this casserole comes from the Italian sausage. Most brands have sausages ranging from mild to hot. So the spicier the sausage you choose, the spicier your casserole will be.

Ye New Irish Stew

1	pound boneless lamb, cut into ¾-inch pieces
1	medium onion, cut into thin wedges
1	tablespoon instant beef bouillon granules
½	teaspoon dried thyme, crushed
¼	teaspoon dried basil, crushed
1	bay leaf
2	medium potatoes, peeled and quartered
3	medium carrots, sliced ½ inch thick

● In a 3-quart casserole stir together the lamb, onion, bouillon granules, thyme, basil, 1¾ cups *water,* and ½ teaspoon *salt.* Add bay leaf. Micro-cook, covered, on 100% power (HIGH) 7 to 8 minutes or till bubbly; stir. Reduce power to 50% (MEDIUM). Micro-cook, covered, 20 minutes, stirring after 10 minutes.

Stir in the potatoes and sliced carrots. Micro-cook, covered, on 50% power (MEDIUM) about 20 minutes or till lamb is done and vegetables are crisp-tender, stirring once. Remove bay leaf.

Irish peasants originally used goat meat in this hearty stew. Our contemporary version calls for lamb.

| 1 | tablespoon cornstarch |
| 1 | tablespoon cold water |

● Stir together cornstarch and water, then stir into lamb mixture. Micro-cook, uncovered, on 100% power (HIGH) 2 to 3 minutes or till thickened and bubbly, stirring once. Reduce power to 50% (MEDIUM). Micro-cook, uncovered, 2 minutes, stirring every minute. Serves 4.

Zesty Beef Stroganoff

2	pounds boneless beef round steak
2	medium onions, chopped
1	cup water
2	tablespoons cooking oil
2	cloves garlic, minced

● Partially freeze beef. Thinly bias-slice into bite-size strips.

In a 3-quart casserole combine beef, onions, water, oil, and garlic. Micro-cook, covered, on 100% power (HIGH) 5 minutes; stir. Reduce power to 50% (MEDIUM). Micro-cook, covered, 22 to 24 minutes or till beef is tender, stirring after 12 minutes. Skim off fat.

For beef stroganoff with a kick, try our version. We've added chili sauce, chili powder, and soy sauce.

½	cup chili sauce
1	tablespoon paprika
1	tablespoon chili powder
2	teaspoons seasoned salt
1	teaspoon soy sauce
1	8-ounce carton dairy sour cream
3	tablespoons all-purpose flour
1	8-ounce can sliced mushrooms, drained
	Hot cooked noodles
	Snipped chives (optional)

● Stir in the chili sauce, paprika, chili powder, seasoned salt, soy sauce, and ¾ cup *water.* Micro-cook, covered, on 100% power (HIGH) about 4 minutes or till heated through. Combine sour cream and flour. Gradually add about *1 cup* of the hot mixture to the sour cream, then return all to the casserole. Stir in the mushrooms. Micro-cook, uncovered, on 100% power (HIGH) about 6 minutes or till thickened and bubbly, stirring once. Serve over noodles. Sprinkle chives atop, if desired. Makes 8 to 10 servings.

Sweet-and-Sour-Sauced Pork

¾ pound boneless pork 1 tablespoon cooking oil	● Thinly bias-slice pork into bite-size strips. Preheat a 10-inch microwave browning dish on 100% power (HIGH) for 5 minutes. Add oil, then swirl to coat dish. Add pork. Micro-cook, uncovered, on 100% power (HIGH) for 2 to 4 minutes or till no longer pink. Use a slotted spoon to remove pork from the browning dish, reserving juices in the dish. Set pork aside.	**Start with peach or pineapple pie filling. Then stir in some vinegar and soy sauce. You'll get plenty of sweet-and-sour flavor—the easy way!**
1 6-ounce package frozen pea pods 1 cup frozen crinkle-cut carrots	● Thaw pea pods and carrots. In juices in the browning dish micro-cook vegetables, covered, on 100% power (HIGH) for 4 to 5 minutes or till crisp-tender.	
1 21-ounce can peach *or* pineapple pie filling 3 tablespoons vinegar 3 tablespoons soy sauce 1 teaspoon instant chicken bouillon granules Hot cooked rice	● In a bowl combine pie filling, vinegar, soy sauce, and bouillon granules. Stir pie filling mixture and pork into vegetables. Micro-cook, uncovered, on 100% power (HIGH) for 3 to 5 minutes or till heated through. Serve over rice. Serves 4.	

Gyro Burgers

¼ cup crumbled feta cheese
3 tablespoons fine dry bread crumbs
¼ teaspoon dried oregano, crushed
⅛ teaspoon garlic powder
⅛ teaspoon pepper
1 pound ground lamb *or* beef

● In a mixing bowl combine feta cheese, bread crumbs, oregano, garlic powder, and pepper. Add meat, then mix well. Shape meat mixture into four ½-inch-thick oval-shaped patties.
Place in a 10x6x2-inch baking dish. Cover with waxed paper. Micro-cook patties on 100% power (HIGH) 6 to 8 minutes or till done, turning patties and rotating the dish a half-turn once.

2 large pita bread rounds, halved
¼ cup dairy sour cream
1 cup shredded lettuce
1 small tomato, chopped
¼ cup chopped cucumber
¼ cup sliced pitted ripe olives

● Meanwhile, generously spread inside of pita halves with sour cream. Sprinkle some of the lettuce, tomato, and cucumber into each pita half. Place 1 patty in each pita half. Sprinkle with olives. Makes 4 servings.

To make a true-to-form Greek gyro (pronounced JEE-row or YEE-row) sandwich, you'd use pressed meat that's been grilled on a vertical rotisserie. Our version has the same robust seasonings as the real thing but comes in a burger that's easy to fix.

Open-Face Chili Sandwiches

½ pound ground beef
1 small onion, chopped (¼ cup)

● Crumble beef into a 2-quart casserole, then stir in onion. Micro-cook, covered, on 100% power (HIGH) 4½ to 5½ minutes or till beef is done and onion is tender, stirring once to break up meat.

1 8-ounce can red kidney beans, drained
1 8-ounce can tomato sauce
1½ teaspoons chili powder
¼ teaspoon salt
4 hamburger buns, split
1 cup shredded cheddar cheese (4 ounces)
1 cup shredded lettuce (optional)
¼ cup dairy sour cream (optional)

● Stir kidney beans, tomato sauce, chili powder, and salt into beef mixture. Micro-cook, covered, on 100% power (HIGH) about 4 minutes or till heated through, stirring once. Place 1 halved bun, cut side up, on each of 4 individual plates. Spoon some of the beef mixture atop both halves of each bun. Sprinkle with cheese. If desired, top with lettuce and sour cream. Makes 4 servings.

For the real chili enthusiast who craves chili in any shape or form, here's a mildly spicy version served on a bun.

Knackwurst In Beer

1 cup beer
1 tablespoon brown sugar
1 tablespoon soy sauce
1½ teaspoons prepared mustard
½ teaspoon chili powder
1 clove garlic, minced
  Few dashes bottled hot pepper sauce
4 5-inch links fully cooked knackwurst *or* smoked bratwurst

● For marinade, in a 2-cup measure combine beer, brown sugar, soy sauce, mustard, chili powder, garlic, and hot pepper sauce.
  Cut deep diagonal slits 1 inch apart in each sausage link, cutting to, but not through, the opposite side. Place sausages in a shallow 8x8x2-inch baking dish. Pour marinade over sausage links. Cover and refrigerate several hours or overnight, spooning marinade over sausage occasionally.

4 individual French rolls
1 8-ounce can sauerkraut, drained
½ cup shredded carrot

● Cut rolls in half lengthwise, then hollow out rolls, leaving ¼-inch shells. (Save excess bread for another use.) Set shells aside. Remove sausages from marinade. Stir sauerkraut and carrot into marinade. Return sausages to baking dish. Micro-cook, uncovered, on 100% power (HIGH) 8 to 10 minutes or till heated through. Use a slotted spoon to fill each roll with some of the sauerkraut mixture, then top with a sausage and the roll top. Makes 4 servings.

The marinade has a real kick. That's why you cut deep slits in the knackwurst—to let all that good flavor seep into the sausage.

Fiesta Pitas

1 small *or* ½ of a medium avocado, pitted, peeled, and chopped
1 small tomato, seeded and chopped
2 tablespoons taco sauce
1 tablespoon sliced green onion

● For avocado salsa, in a small bowl stir together avocado, tomato, taco sauce, onion, and ⅛ teaspoon *salt.* Cover and chill till ready to use.

1 beaten egg
2 tablespoons taco sauce
2 tablespoons regular rolled oats
2 tablespoons diced green chili peppers
1 teaspoon chili powder
½ teaspoon salt
¾ pound ground beef

● In a medium mixing bowl stir together egg and taco sauce. Stir in oats, chili peppers, chili powder, and salt. Add ground beef, then mix well. Shape mixture into four ½-inch-thick patties. Place patties in an 8x8x2-inch baking dish. Cover with waxed paper. Micro-cook on 100% power (HIGH) 4 to 6 minutes or till done, turning patties and rotating the dish a half-turn once.

2 large pita bread rounds, halved
4 lettuce leaves
  Black olives (optional)

● Line each pita half with a lettuce leaf. Cut each burger in half. Place 2 burger halves in each pita half. Top with some of the avocado salsa. Garnish with black olives, if desired. Makes 4 servings.

Break out of the same-old-sandwich rut. Try this snazzy rendition of the all-American hamburger hit. The spicy burger comes in a pita, and an avocado-and-tomato salsa adds to its fiesta flair.

Photo-Finish Turkey Loaf

1 beaten egg
1 cup soft bread
    crumbs (1½ slices)
½ cup alfalfa sprouts,
    snipped
1 small green pepper, finely
    chopped (⅓ cup)
1 tablespoon dried minced
    onion
¼ teaspoon ground ginger
¼ teaspoon salt
¼ teaspoon pepper
1 pound ground raw turkey
	● In a medium mixing bowl stir together the egg, bread crumbs, alfalfa sprouts, green pepper, onion, ginger, salt, and pepper. Add ground turkey. Mix well.
	    In a 9-inch microwave-safe pie plate shape turkey mixture into a 6-inch ring, with a 2-inch hole in the center.

Sweet-and-sour barbecue sauce	● Micro-cook, covered loosely with waxed paper, on 100% power (HIGH) for 7 to 9 minutes or till turkey is no longer pink, giving dish a quarter-turn every 3 minutes. Drizzle meat with *about ¼ cup* of the barbecue sauce. Let stand for 5 minutes. Transfer to a serving plate. Pass additional barbecue sauce. Serves 4.

You'll be first under the wire when this high-performance meat loaf is your entry in the race to beat the mealtime clock.

Turkey Cassoulet

½ pound ground raw turkey 1 medium onion, chopped (½ cup) ¼ teaspoon garlic powder	● In a 1½-quart casserole crumble ground turkey. Add onion and garlic powder. Micro-cook, covered, on 100% power (HIGH) for 3 to 5 minutes or till turkey is no longer pink, stirring once to break up meat. Drain.

½ pound smoked turkey
    sausage, cut into
    ½-inch pieces
1 15-ounce can great
    northern beans
1 8-ounce can tomato sauce
½ teaspoon instant beef
    bouillon granules
¾ teaspoon dried thyme,
    crushed
¼ teaspoon pepper
1 bay leaf
	● Stir in sausage pieces, *undrained* beans, tomato sauce, bouillon granules, thyme, pepper, and bay leaf. Micro-cook, covered, on 100% power (HIGH) for 6 to 8 minutes or till heated through, stirring twice. Remove bay leaf. Serves 4.

Determining the composition of the true French cassoulet is impossible because ingredients vary from region to region. But you'll find our turkey version continues in the best tradition of this hearty stew.

Photo-Finish Turkey Loaf

Creole-Style Chicken

1 **medium green pepper, chopped (¾ cup)** 1 **medium onion, chopped** 1 **tablespoon butter *or* margarine** 1 **clove garlic, minced**	● In a 2-quart casserole micro-cook pepper, onion, butter or margarine, and garlic, covered, on 100% power (HIGH) for 2 to 3 minutes or till onion is tender.
1 **14½-ounce can tomatoes, cut up** 1½ **cups cooked chicken** ½ **of a 6-ounce can (⅓ cup) tomato paste** ½ **teaspoon chili powder** ¼ **teaspoon sugar** ¼ **teaspoon salt** ¼ **teaspoon ground red pepper** ¼ **teaspoon dried thyme, crushed** ¼ **teaspoon cracked black pepper**	● Stir in *undrained* tomatoes, chicken, tomato paste, chili powder, sugar, salt, red pepper, thyme, and pepper. If desired, cover and refrigerate casserole for 3 to 24 hours.
Hot cooked rice	● Before mealtime, micro-cook, covered, on 100% power (HIGH) for 7 to 8 minutes or till heated through, stirring twice. Serve over rice. Makes 4 servings.

Creole cooks combine the best of Spanish and French cuisines, then add the fresh ingredients from Louisiana and other Gulf States—truly a melting pot of culinary influences.

Chicken Couscous

1 **medium onion, thinly sliced and separated into rings** 2 **medium carrots, thinly sliced (1 cup)** 2 **tablespoons butter *or* margarine** 2 **cloves garlic, minced**	● Place the onion, carrots, butter or margarine, and garlic in a 12x7½x 2-inch baking dish. Cover with vented clear plastic wrap. Micro-cook on 100% power (HIGH) for 5 minutes, stirring once. Remove from the baking dish and set aside.
6 **chicken thighs** 2 **teaspoons chili powder** ¾ **teaspoon ground ginger** ¾ **teaspoon ground cumin**	● In the same baking dish arrange chicken, skin side down, with meatiest portions toward outside of the dish (see photo, page 22). Cover with vented clear plastic wrap. Micro-cook on 100% power (HIGH) for 9 minutes, rotating the dish a half-turn after 5 minutes. Remove chicken. Drain fat. In a small bowl combine chili powder, ginger, and cumin.
1 **14½-ounce can stewed tomatoes, cut up** 1 **stalk celery, cut into 1-inch pieces** ½ **cup water**	● Return carrot mixture to the baking dish. Stir in *undrained* tomatoes, celery, water, and *half* of the spices. Arrange chicken, skin side up, in the dish with meatiest portions to outside of the dish. Sprinkle remaining spices over chicken. Cover with vented clear plastic wrap. Micro-cook on 70% power (MEDIUM-HIGH) for 20 to 25 minutes or till chicken is done, basting chicken and giving the dish a half-turn *every* 10 minutes.
1½ **cups ready-to-cook couscous** ¼ **cup snipped parsley (optional)**	● Meanwhile, prepare the couscous according to package directions. Stir in parsley, if desired. Spoon couscous onto a large platter. Arrange chicken atop. Use a slotted spoon to place vegetables atop, reserving juices. Keep warm.
2 **tablespoons cold water** 2 **tablespoons cornstarch** ½ **cup raisins** ½ **cup peanuts**	● Skim fat from reserved juices. Pour into a 4-cup glass measure. Stir together water and cornstarch. Stir into juices. Micro-cook, uncovered, on 100% power (HIGH) for 2 to 3 minutes or till thickened and bubbly, stirring every minute. Stir in raisins and peanuts. Spoon atop chicken. Makes 6 servings.

Just saying the word couscous (pronounced KOO-skoos) conjures up images of exotic places. This steamed coarsely ground wheat (semolina) is typical of dishes served in Morocco, Algeria, and Tunisia. Look for couscous in your grocery or health food store.

Wheat 'n' Nut Chicken

⅓ cup ground walnuts *or* pecans
2 tablespoons wheat germ
1 tablespoon all-purpose flour
¼ teaspoon salt
¼ teaspoon pepper

● In a shallow dish or pie plate stir together ground walnuts or pecans, wheat germ, flour, salt, and pepper.

Soggy chicken puts a damper on any meal, so our Test Kitchen developed a new way to crisp-cook coated chicken in the microwave oven. To keep the coating crisp, coat only three sides of the chicken pieces, then cook them, uncoated side down, on a microwave-safe rack

2 to 2½ pounds meaty chicken pieces (breasts, wings, thighs, and drumsticks)
1 tablespoon milk

● On waxed paper brush each chicken piece with milk. Roll pieces in nut mixture to coat on *three* sides.

● In a 12x7½x2-inch baking dish arrange pieces on a microwave-safe rack with *uncoated* side down and the meatiest portions toward the outside of the dish (see photo, below). Sprinkle and pat on any remaining coating. Micro-cook, covered loosely with paper towels, on 100% power (HIGH) for 12 to 14 minutes or till chicken is no longer pink, rearranging the pieces after half of the cooking time. Makes 4 servings.

Arranging the chicken pieces with the meatiest portions toward the outside of the dish helps ensure even cooking in the microwave oven.

Five-Spice Sesame Chicken

12 sesame toast crackers,
  crushed (½ cup)
 1 tablespoon sesame seed
 ½ teaspoon five-spice
  powder
 ¼ teaspoon salt
 ¼ teaspoon paprika

● For coating, in a shallow dish combine crushed crackers, sesame seed, five-spice powder, salt, and paprika.

Because five-spice powder is basically a blend of five spices, it's easy to make your own if you have the ingredients and a few minutes to spare.

 2 to 2½ pounds meaty
  chicken pieces (breasts,
  wings, thighs, and
  drumsticks)
 2 tablespoons milk

● On waxed paper brush each chicken piece with milk. Roll pieces in coating mixture to coat on *three* sides.

In a 12x7½x2-inch baking dish arrange chicken pieces on a microwave-safe rack with *uncoated* side down and the meatiest portions toward the outside (see photo, opposite). Micro-cook, loosely covered with paper towels, on 100% power (HIGH) for 12 to 14 minutes or till chicken is no longer pink, rearranging the pieces after half of the cooking time. Makes 4 servings.

Just combine 1 teaspoon ground *cinnamon*, 1 teaspoon crushed *aniseed*, ¼ teaspoon crushed *fennel seed*, ¼ teaspoon ground *pepper*, and ⅛ teaspoon ground *cloves*. Store in a tightly covered container.

Or, if you prefer, look for five-spice powder in the Oriental foods section of your grocery store.

Attention, Microwave Owners

Our recipes were tested in countertop microwave ovens that provide 600 to 700 watts of cooking power. Cooking times are approximate because microwave ovens vary by manufacturer. If your oven has fewer watts, foods may take a little longer to cook.

Honey of a Chicken

½ teaspoon finely shredded
  orange peel
½ cup orange juice
2 tablespoons honey
1 tablespoon soy sauce
2 teaspoons cornstarch

● For sauce, in a 2-cup measure stir to-gether orange peel, orange juice, honey, soy sauce, and cornstarch.

Micro-cook, uncovered, on 100% pow-er (HIGH) for 2 to 3 minutes or till sauce is thickened and bubbly; stir every minute. Set aside.

2 to 2½ pounds meaty
  chicken pieces (breasts,
  wings, thighs, and
  drumsticks)

● In a 12x7½x2-inch baking dish ar-range chicken, skin side down, with meatiest portions toward the outside. Mi-cro-cook, covered loosely with waxed pa-per, on 100% power (HIGH) for 9 minutes, giving dish a half-turn and re-arranging chicken once. Drain well.

Brush chicken with sauce. Turn chick-en; brush with sauce again. Micro-cook, covered, on 100% power (HIGH) for 8 to 10 minutes or till chicken is no longer pink. Remove from oven; keep warm. Reheat remaining sauce, uncovered, for 1 minute. Pass with chicken. Serves 4.

Micro-Plus Grilled Chicken: Prepare as above, *except* after micro-cooking chicken for 9 minutes, transfer to a pre-heated grill. Arrange chicken, skin side down, directly over *medium* coals. Brush with sauce and grill for 10 minutes. Turn; brush with sauce. Grill for 8 to 10 minutes more or till chicken is done, brushing several times with sauce.

Spinach Tomatoes

1	**10-ounce package frozen chopped spinach**
¾	**pound ground raw turkey**

● In a 1-quart casserole micro-cook spinach, covered, on 100% power (HIGH) for 7 minutes; stir once. Drain; squeeze out excess water. Set aside.

In the same dish crumble ground turkey. Micro-cook, covered, on 100% power (HIGH) for 3 to 5 minutes or till meat is no longer pink, stirring once. Drain.

4	**large tomatoes**
1	**beaten egg**
¼	**cup fine dry Italian-seasoned crumbs**
¼	**cup grated Parmesan cheese**
¼	**teaspoon onion powder**
¼	**teaspoon dried oregano, crushed**

● Meanwhile, cut a ¼-inch slice off the top of each tomato. Scoop out the tomato pulp, leaving a ¼-inch shell. Invert on paper towels to drain.

In a medium mixing bowl stir together egg, bread crumbs, Parmesan cheese, onion powder, oregano, and ¼ teaspoon *pepper*. Stir in turkey and spinach.

Salt and pepper
Parmesan cheese

● Sprinkle insides of tomato shells with salt and pepper. Fill each with some of the turkey mixture. Top with Parmesan cheese. Place in an 8x8x2-inch baking dish. Micro-cook, uncovered, on 100% power (HIGH) 4 to 6 minutes or till heated through, giving dish a half-turn once. Serves 4.

Cranberry-Raisin-Sauced Chicken

2 whole large skinned and boned chicken breasts, halved lengthwise	● Place chicken pieces in a 10x6x2-inch baking dish. Micro-cook, covered loosely with waxed paper, on 100% power (HIGH) for 4 to 6 minutes or till no longer pink, turning pieces over and re-arranging once. Drain. Keep warm.
1 8-ounce can whole cranberry sauce ¼ cup raisins 1 tablespoon brown sugar Dash ground cloves	● In a 2-cup measure combine cranberry sauce, raisins, brown sugar, and cloves. Micro-cook, uncovered, on 100% power (HIGH) for 1 to 2 minutes or till heated through, stirring once. Serve sauce over chicken. Serves 4.

You'll be the quickest draw in the kitchen when you serve up this saucy chicken dish. Tart cranberries teamed with sweet raisins and a dash of spice will soon have it on your family's most-wanted list.

Coriander Chicken

1 tablespoon butter *or* margarine 1 teaspoon lemon juice 1 teaspoon ground coriander ¼ teaspoon onion powder ⅛ teaspoon chili powder	● In an 8x8x2-inch or 10x6x2-inch baking dish combine butter or margarine, lemon juice, coriander, onion powder, and chili powder. Micro-cook, uncovered, on 100% power (HIGH) for 45 seconds or till butter or margarine is melted. Stir to mix well.
1 whole large skinned and boned chicken breast, halved lengthwise	● Dip chicken pieces in butter mixture to coat well. Arrange in the dish. Micro-cook, covered loosely with waxed paper, on 100% power (HIGH) for 4 to 6 minutes or till chicken is no longer pink; turn pieces over and rearrange once.
1½ teaspoons all-purpose flour 1 teaspoon brown sugar Dash ground red pepper ¼ cup chicken broth 1 cup cooked vegetables (optional) Lemon slices (optional)	● Transfer chicken to a serving platter, reserving liquid. Keep chicken warm. For sauce, in a 2-cup measure combine flour, brown sugar, and red pepper. Stir in reserved liquid and chicken broth. Micro-cook, covered, on 100% power (HIGH) for 1 to 2 minutes or till the mixture is thickened and bubbly, stirring every 30 seconds. Micro-cook 30 seconds more. Serve over chicken and cooked vegetables, if desired. Garnish with lemon slices, if desired. Serves 2.

Ground coriander is made from the seeds of the Chinese parsley or cilantro plant. The flavor will remind you of a combination of lemon and sage—completely compatible with poultry.

Turkey Enchiladas

½ pound ground raw turkey
1 cup mild salsa
½ cup sliced pitted ripe olives
⅛ teaspoon garlic powder

● In a 1-quart casserole crumble turkey. Micro-cook, covered, on 100% power (HIGH) for 3 to 4 minutes or till no longer pink; stir once. Drain. Stir in salsa, olives, and garlic powder.

1 8-ounce container soft-style cream cheese with chives and onion
6 6-inch flour tortillas
1 cup shredded Monterey Jack cheese *or* cheddar cheese (4 ounces)

● Spread *2 tablespoons* of the cream cheese with chives on *each* tortilla. Spoon *⅓ cup* of the turkey mixture down the center of *each* tortilla. Roll up and place, seam side down, in a greased 10x6x2-inch baking dish. Micro-cook, covered with vented plastic wrap, on 100% power (HIGH) for 4 to 6 minutes or till heated through, giving dish a half-turn once. Top tortillas with cheese. Micro-cook, uncovered, on 100% power (HIGH) for 1 to 1½ minutes more or till cheese melts. Serves 4 to 6.

Our Test Kitchen home economists recommend using the thickest salsa available to help keep the tortillas crisp.

Quick Chicken Saltimbocca

1 whole large skinned and boned chicken breast, halved lengthwise

● Place each chicken piece, boned side up, between 2 pieces of clear plastic wrap. Working from the center to the edges, pound the chicken lightly with the fine-toothed or flat side of a meat mallet, forming a rectangle about ⅛ inch thick. Remove the wrap.

1 2.5-ounce package very thinly sliced turkey ham
1 slice Swiss cheese, halved
½ of a small tomato, peeled, seeded, and chopped
1 tablespoon butter *or* margarine
2 tablespoons fine dry seasoned bread crumbs
Paprika

● For *each* chicken roll, place *half* of the turkey ham on a chicken rectangle, folding ham, if necessary, to fit. Place *one* half slice of Swiss cheese on the ham, near one edge. Top with *half* of the tomato. Fold in sides of chicken and roll up jelly-roll style, starting from edge with cheese (see photo, right).
　In a shallow baking dish micro-cook the butter on 100% power (HIGH) about 20 seconds or till melted. Place chicken rolls, seam side down, in the shallow baking dish. Roll chicken in the melted butter to coat. Sprinkle with bread crumbs and paprika.

Fold the sides of the chicken piece toward the center and then roll it up jelly-roll style.

Tomato slices (optional)
Fresh parsley (optional)

● Micro-cook, uncovered, on 70% power (MEDIUM-HIGH) for 5 to 7 minutes or till chicken is no longer pink, giving dish a half-turn every 2 minutes. Garnish with sliced tomato and parsley sprigs, if desired. Makes 2 servings.

Plum-Good Chicken

⅓ cup plum preserves
2 teaspoons soy sauce
2 to 2½ pounds meaty
   chicken pieces (breasts,
   wings, thighs, and
   drumsticks), skinned
   if desired

● In a small bowl stir together plum preserves and soy sauce. Brush chicken pieces on all sides with plum mixture. Arrange chicken pieces in a 12x7½x2-inch baking dish with the meatiest portions of the chicken toward the outside of dish (see photo, page 22).

Micro-cook, covered loosely with waxed paper, on 100% power (HIGH) for 12 to 14 minutes or till chicken is no longer pink, rearranging pieces and basting with juices after half of the cooking time. Remove chicken from dish, reserving juices. Keep chicken warm.

Don't be surprised to see a rich brown-colored sauce instead of a plum-colored sauce. The soy sauce may disguise the color of the plum preserves, but it certainly enhances the flavor.

¼ cup orange juice
1 tablespoon cornstarch
   Hot cooked rice (optional)

● Pour the reserved juices into a 2-cup measure. Skim fat from juices, if necessary. Combine the orange juice and cornstarch. Stir into reserved juices.

Micro-cook, uncovered, on 100% power (HIGH) for 2 to 3 minutes or till mixture is thickened and bubbly, stirring every 30 seconds. Micro-cook for 30 seconds more. Serve over chicken pieces with rice, if desired. Makes 4 servings.

Mostaccioli Turkey

1½ cups mostaccioli
     (4 ounces)
1 pound turkey breakfast
   sausage
1 small onion, chopped
1 small carrot, shredded
1 7½-ounce can tomatoes,
   cut up
1 6-ounce can Italian-style
   tomato paste
⅔ cup water
⅛ teaspoon garlic powder

● Cook mostaccioli according to package directions. Rinse and drain in a colander. Set aside.

Meanwhile, in a 2-quart casserole, crumble turkey sausage. Add onion and carrot. Micro-cook, covered, on 100% power (HIGH) for 5 to 7 minutes or till sausage is no longer pink and vegetables are crisp-tender; stir twice to break up meat. Drain, if necessary. Stir in *un-drained* tomatoes, tomato paste, water, garlic powder, and cooked mostaccioli.

Cooking pasta in your microwave oven takes about the same time as cooking it conventionally, so we suggest cooking the mostaccioli on your range top. That way, you can prepare the meat and sauce in the microwave and have them ready to layer as soon as the pasta is done.

1 beaten egg
1 cup ricotta cheese *or*
   cream-style cottage
   cheese, drained
¼ cup grated Parmesan
   cheese
½ teaspoon dried oregano,
   crushed

● For the cheese mixture, in a small mixing bowl stir together the egg, ricotta cheese or cottage cheese, Parmesan cheese, and oregano.

Place *half* of the turkey mixture in a 10x6x2-inch baking dish. Spread cheese mixture atop. Top with remaining meat mixture. Micro-cook, covered, on 100% power (HIGH) for 10 to 12 minutes or till warm; give dish a half-turn every 3 minutes. Serves 4.

Christmas Eve Dinner for Four

When the occasion calls for something special, try this light and delicious menu that's as festive as can be yet quick as a wink. Because you prepare most of it in the microwave oven, you can relax and enjoy the good company (see recipes, pages 32–33).

MENU
Tarragon Spinach Salad
Chicken à l'Orange
Rolls with whipped butter
Dutch Apple Cake
White Wine Spritzers

MENU COUNTDOWN
Several Hours Ahead:
Prepare salad dressing for Tarragon Spinach Salad; chill. Wash salad ingredients; chill.

2 Hours Ahead:
Make Dutch Apple Cake.
1 Hour Ahead:
Prepare Chicken à l'Orange. Finish assembling Tarragon Spinach Salad.
At Serving Time:
Prepare White Wine Spritzers.

White Wine Spritzers

Pictured on pages 30–31.

1 750-milliliter bottle dry white wine, chilled
2 cups carbonated water, lemon-lime carbonated beverage, *or* ginger ale, chilled
  Carambola, sliced and seeds removed (optional)

● Just before serving, fill each of 4 glasses two-thirds full of wine. Add enough carbonated water, lemon-lime carbonated beverage, or ginger ale to almost fill glass. Stir gently. Garnish with a slice of carambola on edge of the glass, if desired. Makes 4 servings.

These spritzers feature a wonderfully special garnish—carambola, also called star fruit. The flesh is juicy and may be sweet or sour depending on the variety. No need to peel it. The skin is edible.

Chicken à l'Orange

Pictured on pages 30–31.

½ teaspoon finely shredded orange peel
¾ cup orange juice
1 tablespoon soy sauce
1½ teaspoons cornstarch
¼ teaspoon garlic powder

● For sauce, in a 2-cup measure stir together orange peel, orange juice, soy sauce, cornstarch, and garlic. Micro-cook, uncovered, on 100% power (HIGH) for 2 to 4 minutes or till thickened and bubbly, stirring every minute; set aside.

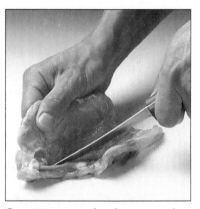

2 whole large chicken breasts (2 pounds total), skinned, boned, and halved lengthwise

● Arrange chicken in a 10x6x2-inch baking dish with meatiest portions to outside of dish (see photo, page 22). Cover with vented clear plastic wrap. Micro-cook on 100% power (HIGH) for 8 to 10 minutes or till just done, turning chicken once. Remove chicken; drain dish.

Save money by boning the chicken breasts yourself. To bone, place the chicken bone side down. Using a sharp knife, cut the meat away from the bone, working from breastbone to the outside. Repeat on other side of breast.

2 medium carrots, cut into julienne strips (1 cup)
2 tablespoons water
1 6-ounce package frozen pea pods

● Place carrots and water in the baking dish. Cover with vented clear plastic wrap. Micro-cook on 100% power (HIGH) about 2 minutes or till almost tender. Add pea pods. Micro-cook on 100% power (HIGH) for 2 to 3 minutes or till pea pods are crisp-tender. Drain.

Orange slices (optional)

● Place chicken atop vegetables. Pour sauce atop. Cover with vented clear plastic wrap. Micro-cook on 100% power (HIGH) for 30 to 60 seconds or till heated through. Garnish with orange slices, if desired. Makes 4 servings.

Tarragon Spinach Salad

Pictured on pages 30–31.

2 tablespoons white wine vinegar 1 tablespoon salad oil 1½ teaspoons snipped fresh tarragon *or* ½ teaspoon dried tarragon, crushed 1 teaspoon sugar ⅛ teaspoon dry mustard	● For dressing, in a screw-top jar combine vinegar, oil, tarragon, sugar, dry mustard, 1 tablespoon *water,* and ⅛ teaspoon *salt.* Cover and shake well. (To store dressing, chill in the refrigerator.)
3 cups torn fresh spinach ¾ cup sliced fresh mushrooms 1 avocado, halved, pitted, peeled, and sliced 1 small onion, sliced and separated into rings	● In a large bowl combine spinach, mushrooms, avocado, and onion. Shake dressing well and pour over salad. Toss lightly to coat. Makes 4 servings.

This versatile vinaigrette dressing complements just about any fresh-vegetable combination.

Dutch Apple Cake

Pictured on pages 30–31.

¼ cup chopped walnuts 1 cup all-purpose flour 1 cup whole wheat flour 1 teaspoon baking powder 1 teaspoon ground cinnamon ½ teaspoon baking soda 2 eggs 1 teaspoon vanilla	● Lightly grease a 10-inch microwave-safe fluted tube pan. Sprinkle walnuts on bottom and sides of the pan. In a large mixing bowl stir together flours, baking powder, cinnamon, baking soda, and ½ teaspoon *salt.* Set aside. In a large mixer bowl combine eggs and vanilla, then beat on high speed of an electric mixer for 2 minutes or till light.
1 cup cooking oil 1 cup packed brown sugar ½ cup sugar 3 medium apples, peeled, cored, and chopped ¾ cup chopped walnuts	● Gradually add oil, beating for 2 minutes or till thick. Gradually beat in sugars. Add dry ingredients alternately with apples and walnuts, beating well on low speed after each addition. Beat at medium speed for 3 minutes. Turn batter into the tube pan.
Cream Cheese Icing (see recipe, right)	● Micro-cook, uncovered, on 50% power (MEDIUM) for 14 to 16 minutes, rotating the pan a quarter-turn every 4 minutes. Rotate the pan again. Micro-cook, uncovered, on 100% power (HIGH) about 1½ minutes or till surface appears nearly dry, rotating a half-turn once. Cool 10 minutes. Invert cake onto a serving plate. Remove pan and cool. Drizzle cake with icing. Serves 10 to 12.

Here's how to make ultra-creamy Cream Cheese Icing: In a small mixer bowl beat together one 3-ounce package softened *cream cheese* and 1 cup sifted *powdered sugar* till fluffy. Beat in ¼ teaspoon *vanilla.* If necessary, beat in enough *milk* (about 1 teaspoon) to make a frosting of spreading consistency. Drizzle over top of cooled cake. If desired, garnish with apple slices, chopped walnuts, and cranberries.

Salmon-Noodle Bake

4 ounces medium whole wheat *or* regular noodles ¼ cup chopped onion ¼ cup chopped green pepper 1 tablespoon butter *or* margarine	● Prepare noodles according to package directions. Drain. Meanwhile, in a 1½-quart casserole micro-cook onion, green pepper, and butter or margarine, covered, on 100% power (HIGH) for 2 to 3 minutes or till onion is tender.
1 3-ounce package cream cheese, softened 1 cup cream-style cottage cheese ¼ cup grated Parmesan cheese ¼ cup milk 1 teaspoon prepared mustard 1 teaspoon Worcestershire sauce ¼ teaspoon dried basil, crushed 1 7¾-ounce can salmon, drained, flaked, and skin and bones removed 2 tablespoons sliced pimiento, drained and chopped	● Add softened cream cheese to the onion mixture, stirring till melted. Stir in cottage cheese, Parmesan cheese, milk, prepared mustard, Worcestershire sauce, and basil. Add the cooked noodles, salmon, and pimiento to mixture, then toss well to coat. Turn into a 10x6x2-inch baking dish. If desired, cover and refrigerate for 3 to 24 hours.
1 tablespoon butter *or* margarine 8 rich round crackers, crushed Parsley (optional) Tomato rose (optional)	● Prepare topper by micro-cooking butter or margarine, uncovered, on 100% power (HIGH) for 30 to 40 seconds or till melted. Toss with crackers. Sprinkle cracker mixture around outer edge of noodle mixture. Micro-cook, uncovered, on 100% power (HIGH) for 12 to 15 minutes or till heated through, rotating the dish once. If desired, garnish with parsley and a tomato rose. Serves 6.

Next time you buy canned salmon, remember this rule of thumb: the redder the flesh, the higher the price. Salmon varieties, from pinkest (least expensive) to reddest (most expensive), are chum, pink, silver, king, chinook, and sockeye. Because you'll mix the ingredients in Salmon-Noodle Bake, the least expensive variety works just fine.

Salmon-Stuffed Zucchini

1 beaten egg
1 teaspoon Worcestershire
    sauce
¾ teaspoon snipped
    dillweed *or* ¼ teaspoon
    dried dillweed
    Dash pepper
1 15½-ounce can salmon,
    drained, flaked, and
    skin and bones removed
½ cup cooked rice

● In a medium mixing bowl combine egg, Worcestershire sauce, dillweed, and pepper. Stir in salmon and cooked rice. Set aside.

Salmon-Stuffed Zucchini is a great choice for the dog days of summer. Dillweed adds light, refreshing summertime flavor. And using your microwave oven means you won't heat up the kitchen.

2 medium zucchini
    (5½ to 6 inches long)
1 small onion, chopped
    (¼ cup)

● Trim ends of zucchini, then halve lengthwise. Scrape out pulp leaving ¼-inch shells. Set shells aside. Finely chop zucchini pulp (should measure about ½ cup). In a medium bowl micro-cook chopped zucchini and onion, covered, on 100% power (HIGH) 1½ to 2 minutes or till onion is tender. Drain. Stir into salmon mixture.

● Place zucchini shells in a 12x7½x2-inch baking dish. Cover with vented clear plastic wrap. Micro-cook on 100% power (HIGH) 2 to 4 minutes or till zucchini are crisp-tender. Place some of the salmon mixture in each zucchini shell. Micro-cook, covered, on 100% power (HIGH) 4 to 6 minutes or till salmon mixture is heated through.

⅓ cup dairy sour cream
1 teaspoon Dijon-style
    mustard
    Dillweed (optional)

● For sauce, in a small bowl stir together sour cream and mustard. Spoon sauce over zucchini. Micro-cook, uncovered, on 100% power (HIGH) 30 to 60 seconds or till sauce is heated through. Garnish with dillweed, if desired. Makes 4 servings.

Tiny Tuna Pockets

1 **8-ounce can crushed pineapple, drained** 1 **3½-ounce can tuna, drained** ½ **cup shredded cabbage** 2 **slices American cheese, torn into pieces** 1 **tablespoon mayonnaise** *or* **salad dressing**	● For filling, in a bowl combine drained pineapple, drained tuna, cabbage, cheese, and mayonnaise or salad dressing.	**Tearing the cheese into pieces saves you the trouble of shredding it.**
2 **small pita bread rounds, cut in half crosswise**	● Spoon filling into pita halves. Place pockets on microwave-safe plate. Microcook pockets on 100% power (HIGH) for 1¼ to 1¾ minutes. Serves 2.	

Get in Step

Your microwave oven is a real time-saver, but you may need to rearrange the work flow so you're ready when your microwave main dish is. Instead of setting the table and preparing a salad or dessert while the microwave recipe cooks, do these tasks first. And be sure everybody is ready to come to the table. Once you pop your dish into the microwave oven, it won't be long before dinner is ready.

Bouillabaisse

10 ounces fresh *or* frozen cod *or* haddock fillets
8 ounces frozen lobster-tail
1 pound fresh *or* frozen shrimp in shells

● In a 3-quart casserole micro-cook fish, if frozen, and lobster, uncovered, on 30% power (MEDIUM-LOW) 4 minutes. Add shrimp, if frozen. Micro-cook, uncovered, on 30% power (MEDIUM-LOW) 11 to 14 minutes or till nearly thawed, separating and rearranging pieces every 4 minutes. Let stand about 5 minutes or till thawed. Shell and devein shrimp. Cut up lobster as shown at right. Cut fish into 1-inch pieces. Set seafood aside.

Use kitchen shears to cut lengthwise through the hard lobster shell. Turn lobster-tail over and cut through underside shell and meat. Cut each halved lobster-tail crosswise through shell and meat three or four times to make six or eight pieces total.

3 medium onions, chopped
2 tablespoons olive oil *or* cooking oil
2 cloves garlic, minced
1 14½-ounce can tomatoes, cut up
1½ cups water
¼ cup snipped parsley
1 teaspoon salt
½ teaspoon finely shredded orange peel
½ teaspoon dried thyme, crushed
¼ teaspoon thread saffron, crushed
¼ teaspoon dried rosemary, crushed
1 pound clams in shells, rinsed

● In the 3-quart casserole micro-cook onions, oil, and garlic, covered, on 100% power (HIGH) 5 minutes, stirring once. Stir in next 8 ingredients and ¼ teaspoon *pepper*. Micro-cook, uncovered, on 100% power (HIGH) 5 to 6 minutes or till bubbly around edges, stirring once. Stir in fish, lobster, shrimp, and clams. Micro-cook, covered, on 100% power (HIGH) 10 to 12 minutes or till fish flakes easily when tested with a fork, stirring 3 times. Serves 4 to 6.

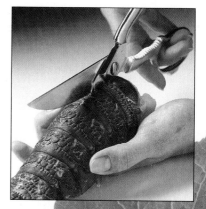

Shrimp with Gruyère Sauce

1½ pounds fresh *or* frozen shrimp in shells	● To thaw shrimp, in a 2-quart casserole micro-cook, uncovered, on 50% power (MEDIUM) about 5 minutes or till nearly thawed, stirring once. Let stand, uncovered, about 6 minutes or till completely thawed. Shell and devein shrimp, then halve lengthwise.	**Sweet and nutlike—that's the flavor of Gruyère cheese. And it makes this shrimp-asparagus dish extra elegant.**
1 10-ounce package frozen cut asparagus, thawed 2 tablespoons water	● In the 2-quart casserole micro-cook shrimp, asparagus, and water, covered, on 100% power (HIGH) for 6 to 8 minutes or till shrimp turn pink and asparagus is crisp-tender. Drain and remove from casserole. Set aside.	
2 tablespoons butter *or* margarine 2 tablespoons all-purpose flour 1 cup light cream *or* milk 1 teaspoon Dijon-style mustard	● For sauce, in the casserole micro-cook butter or margarine, uncovered, on 100% power (HIGH) for 40 to 50 seconds or till melted. Stir in flour. Stir in cream or milk and mustard all at once. Micro-cook, uncovered, on 100% power (HIGH) for 2 to 3 minutes or till thickened and bubbly, stirring every minute.	
½ cup shredded Gruyère cheese (2 ounces) 1 tablespoon lemon juice Hot cooked wild rice *or* long grain rice Paprika (optional)	● Stir in cheese and lemon juice till cheese is melted. Stir in shrimp and asparagus. Micro-cook, uncovered, on 100% power (HIGH) for 1 minute or till heated through. Serve over rice. Sprinkle with paprika, if desired. Serves 4.	

Cheesy Quiches

Butter *or* margarine **1 package (6) refrigerated biscuits**	● Grease four 10-ounce custard cups with butter or margarine. Cut *two* of the biscuits into 8 pie-shaped wedges each. Set wedges aside.
	● Roll remaining biscuits into 4- to 5-inch circles. Place *one* circle in each custard cup, pressing the biscuit against the bottom and up the sides of the cup.
3 beaten eggs **1 8-ounce package (2 cups) shredded cheddar cheese**	● In a small bowl combine eggs and shredded cheddar cheese. Spoon *one-fourth* of the egg mixture (about ⅓ cup) into each custard cup.
Paprika or chili powder (optional)	● Arrange *four* biscuit wedges on top of each custard cup. Sprinkle wedges with paprika or chili powder, if desired.
	● Arrange custard cups in a circle in the microwave oven. Micro-cook, uncovered, on 100% power (HIGH) for 4 to 6 minutes or till edges are set, rearranging custard cups once. Let quiches stand for 5 minutes before serving. Makes 4 servings.

When the quiches have finished cooking, the cheesy filling will be firm around the edges, but it will still jiggle slightly at the center.

Twisty Macaroni and Cheese

1 cup corkscrew *or* elbow macaroni
1 5-ounce jar American cheese spread
¼ cup milk

● Cook macaroni according to package directions; drain.
　In a 1½-quart casserole combine cheese spread and milk. Micro-cook, covered, on 100% power (HIGH) for 2 to 3 minutes or till mixture is melted and smooth, stirring once.

● Stir the drained cooked macaroni into the cheese mixture. Micro-cook, covered, on 100% power (HIGH) for 3 to 4 minutes or till mixture is heated through. Makes 4 servings.

If you can't eat all the macaroni and cheese at once, cover and chill it for later. To reheat the leftovers, micro-cook each ⅔-cup serving, uncovered, on 100% power (HIGH) for 45 seconds to 1 minute or till hot.

Macaroni and Beer-Cheese Sauce

1 cup elbow macaroni
¼ cup finely chopped onion
¼ cup finely chopped green pepper
2 tablespoons butter *or* margarine

● Prepare macaroni according to package directions. Drain and set aside. In a 1½-quart casserole micro-cook onion, pepper, and butter or margarine, uncovered, on 100% power (HIGH) for 2 to 3 minutes or till onion is tender.

4 teaspoons all-purpose flour
1 teaspoon instant beef bouillon granules
¼ teaspoon pepper
¾ cup milk

● Stir in flour, bouillon granules, and pepper, then stir in milk all at once. Micro-cook, uncovered, on 100% power (HIGH) for 3 to 4 minutes or till thickened and bubbly, stirring every minute.

1½ cups shredded American cheese (6 ounces)
¼ cup beer
Few dashes bottled hot pepper sauce
1 medium tomato, chopped (½ cup)
1 tablespoon snipped parsley (optional)

● Stir in cheese, beer, and hot pepper sauce. Stir in macaroni and tomato. Micro-cook, covered, on 70% power (MEDIUM-HIGH) for 4 to 5 minutes or till heated through. Sprinkle with parsley, if desired. Makes 3 servings.

Macaroni and cheese gets a new lease on life with this spicy, beer-cheese sauce. It'll set your palate hoppin'!

Chilies and Cheese Rice

1 medium onion, chopped (½ cup)
1 small green pepper, cut into ¾-inch pieces
1 tablespoon butter *or* margarine
1 clove garlic, minced

● In a 1½-quart casserole combine the onion, pepper, butter or margarine, and garlic. Micro-cook, covered, on 100% power (HIGH) 2 minutes.

1 15-ounce can red kidney beans, drained
1 14½-ounce can tomatoes, cut up
1 cup quick-cooking rice
1 4-ounce can diced green chili peppers, drained
1 teaspoon chili powder
1 cup shredded American cheese (4 ounces)
1 medium tomato, thinly sliced and halved (optional)
Dairy sour cream (optional)

● Stir in kidney beans, *undrained* tomatoes, *uncooked* rice, chili peppers, and chili powder. Micro-cook, covered, on 100% power (HIGH) 14 to 16 minutes or till rice is tender, stirring twice. Stir in cheese. If desired, arrange tomato slices atop rice mixture. Micro-cook, covered, on 100% power (HIGH) 1 minute more. Serve with sour cream, if desired. Makes 4 servings.

When time's ticking away, shredding cheese can be a real hassle. Plan ahead for those precious moments. When you have time, shred a block of cheese all at once. Then store it, tightly wrapped, in ½- or 1-cup portions for a week in the refrigerator or for six months in the freezer.

Letting Off Steam

Covering foods makes microwave cooking even faster because the steam that builds up under the cover helps cook the food. Covering also keeps the food from drying out and eliminates spattering.

Microwave-safe clear plastic wrap is a great cover for dishes you cook in the microwave oven. Microwave-safe plastic wraps withstand microwave temperatures well, as long as they don't come in contact with the hot food. Some plastic wraps are so good at their job, however, that they form a nearly airtight seal with the edge of the dish. To avoid a blowup when steam builds up in the dish and possible burns that may result, vent the clear plastic wrap so steam escapes. Just fold back a small area of the plastic wrap at the edge of the baking dish.

Velvety Cheese Soup

3 tablespoons butter *or* margarine ¼ cup all-purpose flour 2 cups milk 1 10¾-ounce can condensed chicken broth	● In a 2-quart casserole micro-cook the butter or margarine, uncovered, on 100% power (HIGH) for 45 to 60 seconds or till melted. Stir in flour. Stir in milk and chicken broth. Micro-cook, uncovered, on 100% power (HIGH) for 7 to 8 minutes, stirring after every minute.	We discovered it was easier to cut the cheese into chunks if we dipped the knife into cold water before cutting.
1 8-ounce package cheese spread, cut into ½-inch cubes 8 saltine crackers, rich round crackers, *or* melba toast rounds	● Set aside *eight* of the cheese cubes. Stir remaining cheese cubes into the hot mixture. Micro-cook, uncovered, on 100% power (HIGH) for 1 to 2 minutes or till cheese is melted, stirring once. To serve, ladle the soup into 4 microwave-safe soup bowls. Put 2 crackers on the soup in each bowl. Place one of the reserved cheese cubes on each cracker. If desired, melt cheese cubes by micro-cooking each bowl of soup, uncovered, on 100% power (HIGH) for 30 seconds. Makes 4 servings.	

Cheese Manicotti

4 manicotti shells 1 cup cottage cheese	● Cook manicotti according to package directions. Rinse with cold water. Drain and set aside. Place cottage cheese in a food processor bowl or blender container. Cover and process till smooth.	Using a small spoon makes it easier to fill the manicotti shells.
1 beaten egg ½ cup herb-seasoned stuffing mix 1 2-ounce can mushroom stems and pieces, drained 2 tablespoons chopped green pepper 1 tablespoon grated Parmesan cheese 1 tablespoon snipped parsley 1½ teaspoons snipped chives ½ cup tomato sauce ¼ teaspoon garlic powder ¼ teaspoon Italian seasoning 2 teaspoons snipped chives	● In a mixing bowl stir together the egg, stuffing mix, mushrooms, green pepper, Parmesan cheese, parsley, and chives. Stir in cottage cheese. Spoon *one-fourth* of the cheese mixture into each manicotti shell. Place in a 10x6x2-inch baking dish. In a small bowl stir together the tomato sauce, garlic powder, and Italian seasoning. Pour over filled shells. Sprinkle with chives. Cover the baking dish with vented clear plastic wrap.	
	● Micro-cook on 50% power (MEDIUM) for 8 to 10 minutes or till manicotti are heated through. Makes 4 servings.	

Sunshine
In a Pocket

6 beaten eggs ⅓ cup milk ¼ teaspoon salt ¼ teaspoon pepper	● In a 1-quart casserole combine eggs, milk, salt, and pepper. Micro-cook, uncovered, on 100% power (HIGH) for 4 to 5 minutes, pushing the cooked egg to the center of the casserole after each minute.	**The eggs should still be a little runny when you add the cheese. They'll finish cooking while the cheese is melting.**
3 slices American cheese, torn into small pieces	● Sprinkle cheese over the eggs. Micro-cook, uncovered, on 100% power (HIGH) for 1 to 2 minutes or till melted, stirring once.	
2 large pita bread rounds, halved crosswise 1 medium tomato, chopped Alfalfa sprouts	● To serve, place about ½ cup of egg mixture in each pita bread half. Top filled pockets with tomato and alfalfa sprouts. Makes 4 servings.	

Egg 'n' Muffin
Stack

1 teaspoon butter or margarine 1 beaten egg	● In a 10-ounce custard cup micro-cook butter or margarine, uncovered, on 100% power (HIGH) for 15 seconds. Add the beaten egg; micro-cook, uncovered, on 100% power (HIGH) for 45 seconds.	**This hearty breakfast stack is so easy, you can make one in less time than it takes to drive to a fast-food restaurant.**
1 English muffin, split 1 slice boiled ham 1 slice American cheese	● Put the bottom half of the muffin onto a microwave-safe plate. Top with the ham slice, folding or tearing it to fit. Slide the egg out of the custard cup onto the ham. Put the cheese on top.	
	● Micro-cook stack, uncovered, on 100% power (HIGH) for 15 to 20 seconds or till the cheese starts to melt. Top with remaining muffin half. Makes 1.	

Log and Barrel Scramble

1½ cups frozen fried potato nuggets	● In a 9-inch microwave-safe pie plate micro-cook potato nuggets, uncovered, on 100% power (HIGH) for 4 to 5 minutes or till nuggets are hot. Remove nuggets from pie plate and set aside.
1 tablespoon butter *or* **margarine** **4 beaten eggs** **¼ cup milk** **1 teaspoon dried parsley flakes** **¼ teaspoon salt** **Dash pepper**	● In the same pie plate micro-cook the butter or margarine, uncovered, on 100% power (HIGH) for 15 to 30 seconds or till melted. In a small bowl combine the eggs, milk, parsley, salt, and pepper. Pour over melted butter in the pie plate.
2 fully cooked smoked sausage links, sliced	● Add sliced sausage to the egg mixture. Micro-cook, uncovered, on 100% power (HIGH) for 3 minutes, pushing uncooked egg to the center of the dish after every minute.
	● Arrange potato nuggets around the edge of the pie plate. Micro-cook, uncovered, on 100% power (HIGH) about 1 minute or till eggs are set but still shiny. Makes 4 servings.

Some young taste tasters we know said the sausages reminded them of chopped trees and the potatoes looked like barrels. That's how we came up with the name for this dish.

Ham-Stuffed French Toast

2 slices frozen French toast **Butter** *or* **margarine** **1 slice fully cooked ham** **1 slice Swiss** *or* **American cheese**	● Spread one side of each slice of French toast with butter or margarine. Place 1 slice of French toast, buttered side up, on a microwave-safe plate. Top with ham and cheese. Add the remaining slice of French toast, butter side down.
¼ cup maple-flavored syrup	● Micro-cook stuffed French toast, uncovered, on 100% power (HIGH) for 1 to 2 minutes or till cheese is melted. Micro-cook syrup in a 1-cup measure, uncovered, on 100% power (HIGH) for 30 to 45 seconds or till warm. Serve with French toast. Makes 1 serving.

This quick and easy breakfast is one your kids will rate A+.

Ham and Egg Casserole

1 6¾-ounce can chunk-style ham, drained and flaked
1 4-ounce can sliced mushrooms, drained
6 beaten eggs
⅓ cup milk
2 tablespoons grated Parmesan cheese
1 teaspoon dried parsley flakes
½ teaspoon onion powder
⅛ teaspoon pepper

● In a 1½-quart casserole mix the ham and mushrooms. In a bowl combine the eggs, milk, Parmesan cheese, parsley flakes, onion powder, and pepper.

Just serve warm muffins and orange juice with this hearty egg recipe and you've got the perfect Sunday brunch.

● Pour the egg mixture evenly over the ham mixture in the casserole. Micro-cook, uncovered, on 100% power (HIGH) for 4 to 6 minutes or till the egg mixture is almost set, pushing cooked egg to the center of the casserole several times during cooking.

1 cup shredded mozzarella cheese (4 ounces)

● Sprinkle with shredded cheese. Let stand for 5 minutes before serving. Makes 6 servings.

Eggs Done Right

To avoid tough eggs, thoroughly beat the egg yolk and white together before cooking recipes such as Ham and Egg Casserole in the microwave oven.

If the yolk and white aren't thoroughly mixed, the yolk portions will cook faster and become tough before the white portions are done.

Index